BIG DIG

AMASING PIECES of the PAST

Written by Kris Hirschmann
Designed by Joey Gomez
Cover and package design by Bill Henderson

Tangerine Press

an imprint of

SCHOLASTIC

www.scholastic.com

Scholastic and Tangerine Press and associated logos are trademarks of Scholastic Inc

Published by Tangerine Press, an imprint of Scholastic Inc.,
557 Broadway, New York, NY 10012

10 9 8 7 6 5 4 3 2 1

ISBN: 978-0-545-73451-6

Printed and bound in Guangzhou, China

Photo Credits:

BOX

Photograph ©: Delia Castro: Coprolite; iStockphoto/sbayram: background.

BOOK

Photographs ©: 123RF/Linda Bucklin: 6 main; Delia Castro: 28, 29 main; Getty Images/Field Museum Library, by John Gurche: 6 background, 7; iStockphoto: 2 bottom and borders throughout (aloha_17), 8 background (Andrew_Howe), 4 (AntonBalazh), 24 bottom (benedek), 14 top (BertBeekmans), 17 top (bethnewt), 19 top, 19 center (Big_Ryan), 24 top (Bryngelzon), 12, 13 (buradaki), 3 center right, 9 right (CoreyFord), 3 bottom right (CSA-Images), 23 top (drduey), 15 right (Dreamframer), 25 bottom (Elenarts), 10 (emyerson), 22 top (ivan-96), 26 top (jgareri), 29 ruler (joebelanger), 11 silhouettes, 22 bottom (JoeLena), 18 bottom, 19 bottom, 26 bottom, 27 top (KeithBishop), 3 top right, 32 top (leonello), 3 bottom left, 14 right, 15 main, 32 bottom right (LeventKonuk), 2 top, 3 top left, 9 left, 32 bottom left (LindaMarieB), 20 (mg7), 30 bottom (microgen), 14 center (mjbs), 21 (oodelay), 2 background and throughout (prmustafa), 27 bottom (Rubberball), 8 main (RyanFaas), cover background (sbayram), 16, 17 bottom (starmaro), 5 (studioworxx), 25 top (track5), 31 top (ttatty), 9 background (TwilightShow).

CAN YOU DIG IT?

Millions upon millions of years ago, Earth was home to many plants and animals that are **extinct** today. How do we know this? By the clues they left behind, of course! These clues are called **fossils**. They are the keys that help us to unlock our planet's ancient past.

The fossil record shows that this ancient past was an incredible time. We know that Earth was once dominated by prehistoric reptiles called **dinosaurs**. Some dinosaurs were about the size of modern-day chickens. Others were unimaginably enormous— even bigger than blue whales, the largest creatures now living! By studying fossils, scientists have been able to learn a lot about the looks, habits, diets, and lifestyles of these amazing animals.

With this book, you can discover these animals, too. First, take a peek into the dinosaur age. Read about the fossils the dinosaurs left behind and what scientists do to find and study them. Then practice the techniques you have learned with the two excavation blocks in this kit. What will you unearth? Like any scientist, you just need to start digging…and see what you can find!

CONTENTS

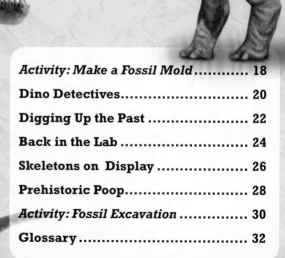

BEFORE THEY WERE FOSSILS

Before we dive into our investigation of fossils, let's back up a few years—4.5 billion of them, to be exact! Around this time, a bunch of rocks and dust clumped together in space to form the planet we now call Earth.

Earth was completely lifeless for a long, long time. It took about a billion years for the first bacteria to form in the planet's seas. It took billions more years for tiny animals to appear. Things moved more quickly after that. Life erupted everywhere, and by about 230 million years ago, dinosaurs were walking the Earth.

The age of dinosaurs is called the Mesozoic Era. The Mesozoic Era is divided into three parts: the Triassic period, the Jurassic period, and the Cretaceous period.

Dinosaurs may have been the most impressive specimens of the Mesozoic Era. They were not the only ones, though. Many new types of mammals, reptiles, fish, insects, and plants emerged during this time. It was a golden age for life on Earth.

DID YOU KNOW?

Modern birds are descended from dinosaurs. Maybe that's why they always stay near the family tree! *GROAN*.

We live in a time called the Cenozoic Era. It started 65 million years ago, when the Mesozoic Era ended. When will the Cenozoic Era end? Good question. No one knows yet!

SHIFTING CONTINENTS

When dinosaurs first appeared, all the land on Earth was joined together in one huge continent called Pangea. Two hundred million years ago, Pangea split into the continents now known as Asia, Africa, North America, South America, Europe, Australia, and Antarctica. That's why scientists have found fossils from the same kinds of dinosaurs on different continents. The creatures got separated when the landmasses broke apart.

Triassic Period

(Approximately 251 – 200 million years ago): The first dinosaurs appeared toward the end of this period. Most Triassic dinosaurs were small, quick meat-eaters that walked on their hind legs.

Jurassic Period

(Approximately 200 – 145 million years ago): During this period, dinosaurs definitely dominated! Enormous plant-eaters, vicious meat-eaters, and birdlike dinosaurs roamed the Earth.

Cretaceous Period

(Approximately 145 – 65 million years ago): Flowering plants popped up all over the planet. Plenty of food and a gentle climate encouraged even more dinosaur species to appear. It was the perfect environment for dinosaurs of all shapes, sizes, and habits.

WHEN GIANTS ROAMED THE LAND

You know that dinosaurs once roamed the Earth. But what exactly are dinosaurs? We can get a hint from the word *dinosaur*, which comes from Greek words meaning "terrible lizard." This phrase is misleading, though. Not all dinosaurs were scary, or "terrible," and they definitely weren't lizards. They were reptiles that share some, but not all, of the features of modern reptiles.

Dinosaurs came in many different shapes and sizes. Some were smaller and lighter than a loaf of bread. Others were incredibly huge and heavy. Some walked on two hind legs, while others ambled along on four limbs. Some lived underwater and had bodies adapted for a swimming life.

Dinosaurs did not vary only in their looks. Different species had very different habits, too. Dinosaurs might be **carnivores** (meat-eaters) or **herbivores** (plant-eaters). They could be aggressive or calm; slow-moving or speedy; active during the daytime or nighttime. With their many behaviors, dinosaurs of different types took advantage of Earth's resources in the ways that suited them best.

Let's learn about a few residents of the Mesozoic Era! The next several pages give you the inside scoop on some well-known species.

DID YOU KNOW ?

Scientists have identified about 1,000 different dinosaur species from fossils.

TYRANNOSAURUS REX
Tyrant Lizard King

TYRANNOSAURUS REX lived during the late Cretaceous period, about 85 million to 65 million years ago. This carnivorous monster was one of the biggest beasts ever to walk on two legs. Despite its massive bulk, T. rex was quick and agile enough to catch the other dinosaurs it liked to eat, including Triceratops and Hadrosaurs. This **predator** tipped its mighty torso forward when it walked or ran. It stuck its long, muscular tail out behind for balance.

Built to Eat

The largest T. rex skull fossil ever found was more than 5 feet (1.5 m) long and 3 feet (0.9 m) wide. That's the size of a refrigerator! T. rex's huge head was packed with razor-sharp teeth—as many as 60 at a time. These wicked chompers could grow to be almost 12 inches (0.3 m) long.

Fast Facts
Height: 20 feet (6 m)
Length: 50 feet (15 m)
Weight: 10,000 pounds (4,500 kg)
Location: Western United States and Canada

TRICERATOPS

TRICERATOPS lived about 70 million years ago, during the late Cretaceous period. This creature was twice as big as a modern-day rhinoceros. Despite its bulk, though, Triceratops wasn't usually dangerous. This herbivore had a gentle nature and roamed the land in huge herds of up to 1,000 individuals, grazing on grass and tasty leaves as it traveled. If a large carnivore attacked, though—watch out! Triceratops was big and strong, and it didn't hesitate to defend itself with its strong tail, clawed hooves, and wicked horns.

Fast Facts

Height:	9.5 feet (2.9 m)
Length:	26 feet (7.9 m)
Weight:	14,000 pounds (6,350 kg)
Location:	Western United States and Canada

T. rex vs. Triceratops

Who would win a one-on-one battle between a T. rex and a Triceratops? Scientists are convinced that the Triceratops would have come out on top! They believe this because they have found Triceratops bones that show signs of damage from T. rex teeth, but which later healed fully. The Triceratops must have killed the T. rex to escape from the deadly encounter.

PTERANODON
"Winged and Toothless"

PTERANODONS are not considered dinosaurs. They belonged to a group of flying reptiles called Pterosaurs. They lived between 83 million and 70 million years ago during the late Cretaceous period. Much like giant pelicans, Pteranodons were fierce meat-eaters who hunted mostly over ocean waters. When a Pteranodon saw prey swimming just below the water's surface, it swooped down and scooped it into its massive beak. Pteranodons had big eyes to help them with this fast-moving task.

Fast Facts

Length:	6 feet (6 m)
Wingspan:	24 feet (7.3 m)
Weight:	35 pounds (16 kg)
Location:	Central United States and England

Catch Me If You Can

Although they were large, Pteranodons were tiny compared to many carnivores of the era. They couldn't have fought off a large, hungry predator. Thanks to their flight skills, though, they didn't need to! Pteranodons were able to glide long distances without landing. They could flap their huge wings for an extra burst of speed if needed. But mostly they just rode the oceanic air currents, relaxed and safe from the many dangers found on land.

APATOSAURUS
"Deceptive Lizard"

APATOSAURUS lived during the Jurassic period, about 154 million to 150 million years ago. One of the largest animals ever to roam the Earth, Apatosaurus lumbered around slowly on four thick, strong legs. It couldn't really outrun predators, but that didn't matter. Apatosaurus was so big that nothing could hurt it! This herbivore probably held its long neck and tail parallel to the ground most of the time, but it could raise its head for short periods to feast from the tallest treetops.

Name That Dino

The name Apatosaurus, which means "deceptive lizard," refers to this dinosaur's history of mistaken identity. Scientists once got it confused with Mosasaurus, a large aquatic reptile. Later, a different scientist unearthed a skeleton that he thought was a brand-new dinosaur species—but it wasn't! It was actually an Apatosaurus skeleton lying next to the skull of a different animal. The scientist named his mixed-up discovery Brontosaurus. It took decades for paleontologists to sort out this colossal confusion.

Fast Facts

Height:	15 feet (4.6 m) at the hip
Length:	85 feet (26 m)
Weight:	36,000 pounds (16,329 kg)
Location:	Western United States

ADOPT A PREHISTORIC PET

Choose a prehistoric animal you would like to adopt. You can use one of the creatures from pages 7 to 10, or you can pick something completely different. Do research in the library or on the Internet to complete the fact sheet for your new pet. Happy hunting!

My Prehistoric Pet

Name:_____

Meaning: _____ Pronunciation: _____
(This means how the name sounds when you say it.)

Discovered or named by:_____ in_____ (year)

Order:_____ Time period: _____

Location: _____

Size:
Length:_____Height:_____Weight:_____

Favorite foods: _____

_____

☐ Carnivore ☐ Herbivore ☐ Both

Fun Facts

1. _____

2. _____

3. _____

WHERE DID THEY GO?

The Mesozoic Era

lasted about 185 million years, give or take a couple million years. That's a *looong* time for one type of creature to rule the Earth.

All good things must come to an end, though, and the dinosaur age was no exception. About 65 million years ago, all of these mighty creatures suddenly died out. Where did they go?

DID YOU KNOW?

No living person has ever seen an actual dinosaur. Humans didn't emerge until about 200,000 years ago. That's way, way, WAY after the dinosaurs died out.

There are two main theories to explain the disappearance of the dinosaurs. Most scientists believe that the extinction was a sudden catastrophe. It occurred after Earth was hit by a huge **asteroid**, or space rock, about 6 miles (10 km) wide. The impact caused a giant cloud of dust to blanket our planet for years, blocking out all sunlight. Most plants and animals, including the dinosaurs, perished in the dark, cold conditions.

The second theory also involves an asteroid, but the reasoning is different. Scientists who believe in a gradual extinction think that Earth's climate changed slowly over a long period. The dinosaurs and other living **organisms** were already in trouble from these changes when the meteorite hit. The effects of the impact were merely the final straw, not the sole cause of the extinction.

DID YOU KNOW?

Scientists think that about 70 percent of all species on Earth, both plant and animal, died out during the Mesozoic-Cenozoic extinction.

A MIGHTY CRATER

Scientists think the Chicxulub (chick-ZULL-ub) Crater in Mexico is the most likely site of the extinction impact. This crater is 110 miles (180 km) wide and 12 miles (20 km) deep. Another suspect is the Shiva Crater along the India-Seychelles rift, which is about 250 miles (400 km) wide and 370 miles (600 km) long. One asteroid could have made both of these craters if it split before impact.

WHAT ARE FOSSILS?

Dinosaurs may have become extinct, but they didn't completely disappear. They left traces of themselves for us to find. These traces are called fossils.

A fossil is any remain or impression preserved from a long-past age. This means that a fossil might look like a bone, a footprint, or even a pile of barf or poop! Just about any dinosaur remains you can imagine have been preserved in fossil form.

So how does it work? Fossilization begins when organic materials are buried in sediment, sand, ash, or mud that settles in the bottom of lakes, swamps, rivers, and other bodies of water. Because they are buried, the organic materials are protected from the elements, and they do not decay.

They get buried deeper and deeper as sediment layers keep collecting and eventually harden into rock.

In the meantime, the original item is going through an amazing change. Water carrying dissolved minerals flows down into the ground. Those minerals seep into tiny holes in the organic material. Sometimes the minerals collect to form a shell around the original material, which then decomposes. At other times, minerals replace the original material bit by bit, preserving its exact shape. Either way, the result is a fossil, a precise copy of something that existed in the distant past.

What Good Are Fossils, Anyway?

Fossils are super important because they teach us about Earth's history. By looking at fossils, scientists can tell what dinosaurs looked like, what animals they hung out with, who and what they ate and who ate them, what kind of parents they were, how they grew, and lots more stuff. We learned everything we know about dinosaurs from the scraps they left behind.

QUICK QUIZ

Scientists have discovered:
A. Fossilized barf
B. Fossilized guts
C. Fossilized blood vessels
D. All of the above

Answer: D

KNOW YOUR FOSSILS

There are five different types of fossils. Each type tells its own story about the past. Check them out and see for yourself!

Petrified Fossils

Petrified fossils are items that have turned to stone. They form when minerals replace part or all of an organism.

Molds and Casts

Molds and casts are not exactly the same, but they are related. A mold forms when an item is pressed into sediment and then dissolves, leaving an impression of its shape behind. A cast forms when minerals and sediment fill the mold, then harden. A cast is the exact opposite of the mold in which it formed.

Carbon Films

All organisms contain an element called carbon. When an organism decays, it can leave a thin film of carbon behind. This carbon is like a photograph and can show an organism's most delicate parts.

Trace Fossils

Trace fossils are fossils that preserve an animal's activity instead of its body. A footprint or a preserved animal burrow are examples of trace fossils.

Preserved Remains

Remains can be preserved if an organism gets trapped in amber (sticky tree sap), tar, or ice. Unlike the other types of fossils, preserved remains are actual, non-petrified parts of the animals or plants to which they belonged.

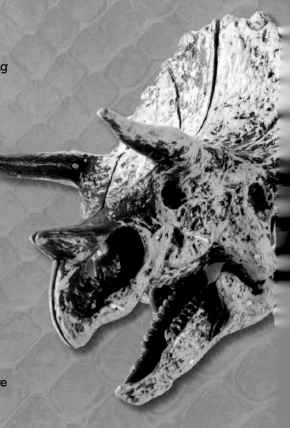

DID YOU KNOW?

More than one million preserved bones have been found in the La Brea Tar Pits in Los Angeles, California. According to scientists, these bones came from 231 different animal species.

MAKE A FOSSIL MOLD

Some fossils form when bones, leaves, and other matter create an imprint on sediment. Over the years, the original matter may disintegrate, but the imprint remains. Create your own decorative fossil mold with this smooth, white dough.

You need:

- 1 cup (130 g) cornstarch
- 2 cups (440 g) baking soda
- 1 cup (240 ml) water
- Toothpick or pencil

What you do:

1. Put the cornstarch and baking soda into a saucepan.

2. Pour the water into the pan. Stir well. With an adult helper, cook the mixture over medium heat until it thickens, about four minutes. (It should look like mashed potatoes.) Remove the saucepan from the heat and pour the mixture onto a plate. Cover with a damp paper towel until it is cool.

3. Knead the dough to make it smooth for shaping.

4. Make a 1-inch (2.5-cm) ball of dough. Flatten the dough on another plate. Choose a fossil design (see pg. 15) and copy it onto your dough by carving with a toothpick or a pencil.

5. Let the dough air-dry for a day. It will be smooth and rock like—great to use as a paperweight!

HELPFUL HINT
Store any unused dough in
an airtight container. Keep it
in the refrigerator until you
are ready to use it.
(mark it DO NOT EAT)

DINO DETECTIVES

You have already learned that fossils are clues to the past. Like all clues, though, fossils can be tricky to figure out. Think about it. Could you tell the difference between a rock-like fossil and a regular rock? Would you even know where to *look* for a fossil? Probably not!

That's where the experts come in. Scientists called **paleontologists** have special training that helps them to find and study fossils. They use their skills to collect information about plants, animals (including dinosaurs), and other organisms that existed in the distant past.

For instance, did a particular dinosaur eat meat or plants? How did it stand and walk? How did it take care of its babies?

A Puzzling Question

Doing this job is not easy. It's like solving a big puzzle without an answer key—and each "puzzle" starts with a question.

LOTS OF WORK

More than 99 percent of all species that have ever lived on Earth are now extinct. This means that there are LOTS and LOTS of ancient organisms to study. It also means that paleontologists won't run out of work anytime soon. Maybe there's a job for you in the future!

DID YOU KNOW? Scientists called **ARCHAEOLOGISTS** do the same general type of work as paleontologists. Instead of looking for ancient plants and animals, though, they focus on ancient human civilizations.

To answer questions like these, paleontologists start with research. They read as much as possible about whatever it is they're interested in. Then they figure out where they should go to look for clues.

In the Field

To find these clues, scientists must leave their labs and search for actual fossils. This part of the job is called working in the field, and it is a huge effort. Paleontologists might have to travel anywhere in the world to reach a research site. Once they get there, they might spend months or even years searching for clues. The process is long, hard, and tiring—but it can also be exhilarating. Most paleontologists say that spending time in the field is their favorite part of the job.

21

DIGGING UP
THE PAST

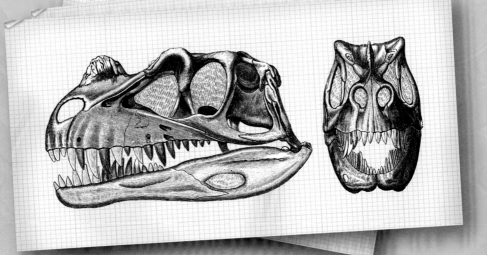

A site where paleontologists are actively looking for fossils is called a dig. The location of a dig depends on what a scientist is hoping to find. If you're looking for T. rex remains, for example, aim your shovel at the western United States and Canada. For birdlike oviraptor fossils, Mongolia's Gobi Desert would be a better bet. Whatever the destination, places where old rocks have been cut open or exposed are a good place to start the search for fossils.

Success! Now What?

WOO-HOO! You've done your homework and you have found a fossil embedded in a rock. Now the real work begins!

Extracting fossils is a long, painstaking process. First, paleontologists protect the dig site with a tent. Then they use special tools to chip the fossil out of the surrounding rock. They work slowly and carefully to avoid damaging the fossil.

While some scientists dig, others do different jobs. They sketch, photograph, and document each discovery with detailed notes. They collect every scrap of information that might end up being a useful clue.

Tools of the Trade

A paleontologist needs special tools on a dig, including:

A geological hammer
Good for breaking rocks apart without breaking what's inside.

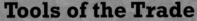

Brushes
Used to whisk dirt away from fossil finds.

Tweezers
For tugging free the tiniest of fossils.

Chisels
Used to chip away rock from the fossils.

A magnifying glass
For getting a close-up look at fossil finds.

23

BACK IN THE LAB

When a dig ends, another part of the paleontologist's job begins. Back in the museum, or in their laboratory, or wherever they take their discoveries, scientists work to figure out what their new fossils mean. They compare them to old ones, or with fossils that other scientists have found.

Careful cleaning is a big part of this process. Cleaning can mean washing with water or using strong chemicals to eat stubborn rock away from fossils. However it's done, scientists must work very slowly so they don't break fragile items or put things together in the wrong order. It can take years to clean and sort all the fossils from a dig.

When the process is finally over, paleontologists share the information they have learned with the scientific community. They are providing a new piece of the puzzle that will help future paleontologists to do their work.

DID YOU KNOW?

Computer programs help paleontologists to draw flesh around fossil fragments. These programs let us "see" into the past.

HOW OLD IS IT?

Scientists use chemicals called potassium and argon to see how old fossils are. Here's how it works: All fossils contain both of these chemicals. As the fossils age, though, the potassium inside them turns to argon. This means that older fossils contain more argon. Sometimes fossil hunters use another method, called carbon-14 dating, to double-check their results. Knowing an item's age lets paleontologists paint a better picture of its origin.

18
Ar
Argon
39.948

19
K
Potassium
39.0983

SKELETONS ON DISPLAY

Most fossils end up cataloged and stored neatly in a box or a cabinet somewhere. The very best fossils, however, get a different treatment. They are prepared and assembled for public display.

Dinosaur skeletons might be the most spectacular of all fossils. These enormous remains help us understand how big dinosaurs really were! They bring the past to life in a way no picture could ever match.

Assembling a dinosaur skeleton takes a lot of work. First, scientists build a frame that's the same shape as the dinosaur to support the bones as they put them in place. The bones are then wired together, and any missing bones are replaced with plastic ones.

Sometimes no real bones have been found for a particular dinosaur. In these cases, a skeleton is constructed of all plastic bones. Either way, the result is what you may have seen in a museum: a complete dinosaur skeleton.

DID YOU KNOW ?

Scientists built the world's first dinosaur skeleton in 1868. The Hadrosaurus skeleton was unearthed in Haddonfield, New Jersey.

A Tyrannosaurus rex skeleton named "Sue" is one of the coolest fossil skeletons ever found. It includes about 80 percent of Sue's bones. The other 20 percent are plastic copies. Today, this mighty specimen stands on permanent display at the Field Museum of Natural History in Chicago, Illinois.

PREHISTORIC POOP

Dinosaurs lived large.

The biggest species could devour incredibly vast amounts of prey or plants in a single feeding session. The end result of all those super-sized meals? You guessed it: Whether you call it poop, scat, feces, turds, or dung, dinosaurs produced huge quantities of it. In fact, scientists believe that the biggest plant-eating dinosaurs may have produced more than 2,000 pounds (4,400 kg) of dung every day!

Most dinosaur poop disintegrated quickly. Some of it, though, has survived to this day in fossilized form. Paleontologists have discovered petrified poop everywhere from England to the Americas and Asia

to Africa. These fossils are called coprolite. They prove that millions of years ago, just like today, what goes in… must come out!

TRUE OR FALSE?

Paleontologists just follow their noses to find coprolite. It smells like…well, like POOP!

False! There is no actual doo-doo in coprolites. Coprolites are petrified fossils, which means that all of the original icky material has been replaced by nice, clean, non-stinky minerals.

DID YOU KNOW?

The biggest coprolite ever found was discovered in Saskatchewan, Canada. The massive mound is 17 inches (43 cm) long and nearly 7 inches (18 cm) wide. Scientists believe that a T. rex was probably responsible for this impressive specimen.

FOSSIL

ACTIVITY: EXCAVATION

This kit comes with two digging blocks that you can excavate, just like a real **PALEONTOLOGIST!** One digging block contains a coprolite or dino poop. The other contains a mystery dinosaur skeleton. You also have a digging tool and a brush. Follow the simple steps on these pages to unearth your buried treasures.

You need:

- Large sheet of white paper
- Digging blocks
- Digging tool
- Brush

What You Do:

1. Spread the paper out on a flat surface. Choose one block and place it in the center of the paper.

2. Using the digging tool, gently scrape away the clay. When you uncover part of an object, keep digging very carefully. Remove all the clay from around the object before taking it out of the block. Keep digging until you have scraped away all of the clay and are left with the pieces of your coprolite or dinosaur fossil.

3. Brush the objects to get rid of any extra clay. If you need to, you can also wash off the remaining clay with water to get your fossils completely clean.

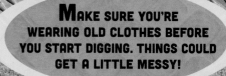

MAKE SURE YOU'RE WEARING OLD CLOTHES BEFORE YOU START DIGGING. THINGS COULD GET A LITTLE MESSY!

IF YOU WANT TO ASSEMBLE YOUR MYSTERY DINOSAUR FOSSIL, YOU'LL NEED TO USE STRONG GLUE. USE THE PICTURE ON PAGE 32 AS A GUIDE. (DON'T LOOK NOW; YOU'LL RUIN THE SURPRISE!) ASK A PARENT TO GLUE THE PIECES TOGETHER FOR YOU. NEVER USE THE GLUE YOURSELF!

Component list
- Wood mallet
- Magnifying glass
- Digging tool
- Brush

WARNINGS!

- Always ask an adult for permission for a safe area to dig your blocks.
- Use in a well-ventilated area.
- Make sure you wear old clothes before you start digging.
- Do not use on finished floors, furniture, or carpet.
- Always cover your area well before starting.
- Wear a safety mask and goggles when chipping blocks.
- Do not to inhale any dust particles.

- Be careful of small pieces that may break off.
- Be careful with chisel point.
- Always chisel away from you, never towards you.
- Be careful with all tools.
- Always clean up your area when you finish.
- Always wash your hands thoroughly with warm soap and water when you finish.
- Keep away from small children.

GLOSSARY

Archaeologist:
A scientist who studies ancient human remains.

Asteroid:
A small rocky body orbiting the sun.

Carnivore:
An animal that eats meat.

Coprolite:
Fossilized feces.

Decompose:
To break down into separate elements.

Dig:
An excavation conducted by a paleontology team.

Dinosaur:
An extinct reptile of the Mesozoic Era.

Extinct:
No longer existing or living.

Fossil:
Preserved evidence of ancient animals or plants.

Fossilization:
The process that turns once-living organisms into fossils.

Herbivore:
An animal that eats plants.

Organic:
Made of materials that come from once-living organisms.

Organism:
A living thing such as a plant, an animal, or a one-celled organism that can function on its own.

Paleontologist:
A scientist who studies organisms that lived in the distant past, mostly by examining fossils.

Predator:
An animal that hunts and eats other animals.